DEVELOPING *female* LEADERS

STUDY GUIDE

KADI COLE

Developing Female Leaders: Study Guide
by Kadi Cole

copyright © 2019, Kadi Cole
ISBN: 978-1-950718-13-9

Contents

Introduction

💡 Big Idea

Though many in church ministry desire for women to be all that God has called them to be, we've often missed the mark in our application. What would the church look like if it were to maximize the influence of our women?

📖 Read

"Welcome" chapter in *Developing Female Leaders*

🎙 Reflect and Discuss

"I realize that females in church leadership is a controversial topic, and although I am not normally one to engage in such an emotionally charged debate, this one continues to bubble up in almost every conversation or leadership engagement I have. Because I come from a spiritually rich and eclectic Christian church background, I have grown to love, understand, and appreciate people and ministries on all sides of this theological issue."

📝 Respond

When it comes to the topic of females in church leadership, what is your theological background? Think about the messages you were taught growing up. Where on the "spectrum" would you say these lessons fall?

_____

_____

_____

_____

As you've grown in your faith, how have your views changed? What new revelations have you discovered?

_____

_____

_____

_____

Whether you're a man or a woman, we've likely all had experiences similar to Kadi's in the beginning of this chapter. What discriminatory language or behavior have you seen, either towards men or women, in the church?

_____

_____

_____

_____

🎙 Reflect and Discuss

"My only intent is to help. If you are someone who is open, curious, hungry, passionate, or perhaps even determined to move this topic forward in your church, I pray this book will serve as a conversation catalyst, a useful tool to help you make changes, and a source of encouragement and inspiration for "what could be.""

📰 Respond

How do you think your location, and the cultural values held in your part of the world, influence your church's beliefs concerning this issue?

_____

_____

_____

_____

What "lovingly ignorant" behaviors have you seen in the church? These are instances wherein people mean well, but aren't wise in their application.

_____

_____

_____

_____

Where on the emotional spectrum do you find yourself today regarding female ministry leadership? Are you curious? Passionate? Numb? Determined? Explain your answer.

_____

_____

_____

_____

What do you hope to get out of reading this book, and working through this study? How do you hope your views, attitudes, and actions are shaped by this experience?

_____

_____

_____

_____

BEST PRACTICE #1:

Seek to Understand

💡 Big Idea

Our upbringing and culture heavily influence what we believe. While these messages can limit our self-worth, there's also potential for good. Many men and women are taking Biblical steps to understand both God's will and the experiences of those around them.

📖 Read

Chapter 1 in *Developing Female Leaders*

🔎 Reflect and Discuss

Kadi spoke with several executive pastors whose hearts were in the right place. They wanted to see women reach their full potential, but didn't know how to go about it. One told her, "There are all these talented women in our congregation, but it's like they can't break through, even as volunteers. We want them to, but we just can't seem to figure it out."

📝 Respond

We are conditioned, specifically in the church, to hold women back from becoming all that God intended. Stereotypes are part of this. What stereotypes permeated your childhood? How were you conditioned to believe certain things based on someone's gender?

_____

_____

_____

_____

Helping women overcome these stereotypes requires that we identify what's holding each woman back. What conversations, or questions, do you need to exchange to empower your female leaders?

_____

_____

_____

_____

🏆 Reflect and Discuss

"Each of us has grown up connecting with some of the stereotypes of our gender and some that do not fit us at all. I know many men who feel insecure that they aren't good at sports or that they can't fix things around the house. What a shame! God hand-makes each one of us and gives us a unique style to fit our specific calling. Stereotypes hurt everyone."

📄 Respond

Above, we explored how stereotypes can be false. However, there can also be an element of truth to them. How have you fit into the stereotypes of your gender?

_____

_____

_____

_____

In the last century alone, drastic changes to women's rights have happened on a national scale. How do you think measures such as giving women the vote, providing maternity leave, and identifying sexual harassment have shaped how the church views female leadership today?

_____

_____

We need both genders serving in all areas of the church. God has given us unique giftings, and a responsibility to live them out. In your church, do both genders feel free to serve in a variety of areas? Explain your answer.

Reflect and Discuss

"The glass ceiling is one thing, but the sticky floor is often just as limiting, especially in ministry circles. These are the attitudes and learned behaviors that women do to themselves that keep them from growing in their leadership abilities and opportunities for advancement."

Respond

Out of cultural conditioning comes "sticky floor" behaviors. How have you seen these behaviors influence the women in your church? Consider Kadi's catalogue of behaviors on pages 11-15 for ideas.

When a job opening arises, women often wait until they are 100% confident of their abilities before applying. How do you think this affects the number of female leaders in today's church?

_____

_____

_____

🎙 Reflect and Discuss

"Take the time to have a conversation with the female leaders you have on your team and in your congregation. Ask them about their stories and how they have impacted their view of themselves as leaders."

📝 Respond

How can you combat the sticky floor behaviors women in your church have adopted, and instill confidence into them?

_____

_____

_____

_____

What questions can you ask to get a better understanding the pasts, beliefs, and reservations of the women you know?

_____

_____

_____

_____

There's a need for men to listen well. There are many men who are seeking out women's perspectives in an effort to learn. If the male church as a whole got better at listening fully to women's perspectives, what effect do you think it would have on church culture?

_____

_____

_____

_____

Whether you're a man or a woman, you likely have at a role model in this area. What characteristics have you witnessed in this person? How does their example inspire you to take the next step?

_____

_____

_____

_____

Clearly Define What You Believe

💡 Big Idea

There's a spectrum of beliefs about female leadership in ministry. The main issue isn't where your church falls on this spectrum, but the gap between your line and where your female leaders *think* your line is. We must clearly define what we believe, both to ourselves and to those we lead.

📖 Read

Chapter 2 in *Developing Female Leaders* and download the Theological Cheat Sheet at *KadiCole.com/Resources*

🔬 Reflect and Discuss

"For a woman who is trying to lead in a church setting, these issues of clarity are often compounded by mixed messages about what, how, and whom she is allowed to lead."

📝 Respond

Have you seen the church give women mixed messages about their role? If so, how do you think this affects their ability to effectively serve?

_____

_____

_____

On the flip side, do you think the church gives men mixed messages about their roles? Explain your answer.

_____

_____

_____

_____

If you could choose one word to describe what it's like to be a female in ministry, what would it be? Why did you choose that word?

_____

_____

_____

_____

⌖ Reflect and Discuss

"Even if you have confidence that your stance is extremely clear, there have likely been mixed messages in how this has played out for [each woman] in your church and in her leadership."

📄 Respond

What has your church done, both in staff settings and from the pulpit, to clarify their stance on female leadership?

_____

_____

_____

_____

Do you think the line is clear for your congregation and staff? Or do you think there needs to be further action to define it?

_____

_____

_____

_____

⚲ Reflect and Discuss

Most godly women are afraid to step over the leadership line, and will stay far below it. This creates the gap between your theological line and where women are comfortable leading. Our goal is to narrow this gap as much as possible.

📝 Respond

Why do you think godly women are overly conservative when it comes to approaching the theological line of leadership?

_____

_____

_____

_____

What risks do women run if they step over the line? How would this affect your church?

_____

_____

_____

_____

What risks do women run if they stay too far below the theological line? How would this affect your church?

_____

_____

_____

_____

Give a brief synopsis of your church's theological line. Where are women allowed to serve?

_____

_____

_____

_____

Now, give a brief summary of where you believe women are comfortable leading at your church. Consider where they're currently leading, and what you've seen and heard from them. Where do your women believe the line is?

_____

_____

_____

_____

What are some concrete ways you can narrow this gap, and empower your women to step all the way up to the Biblical line you've set?

_____

_____

_____

_____

♀ Reflect and Discuss

"Any changes need to be implemented within the style of your church's culture, but the measurement of success will be that your leaders and the majority of your church members understand your beliefs in the same way, and that what they see in the leadership ranks of your church matches what you say you believe."

📝 Respond

Hypocrisy is something with which every Christian—and church—struggles. How have your church's actions diverted from your core beliefs? How have your personal actions contradicted your views on female leadership?

_____

_____

_____

_____

We must make sure our convictions are firmly rooted in Scripture. We can't make lasting, effective change without this foundation. What do you need to do to ensure your convictions are Biblically-based?

_____

_____

_____

_____

Kadi writes, "Don't be afraid to live out your convictions that are clearly based on Scripture, even if it creates some conflict and uncomfortable moments, as God will honor that." Have you ever experienced conflict because you lived out your convictions?

_____

_____

_____

_____

Through Christ, there is infinite grace! We always have the ability to update, amend, and improve our theological stances. How does it make you feel to know that, no matter what, you have space to grow and improve in your beliefs about God?

☻ Reflect and Discuss

Our beliefs about each Person of the Godhead informs what we believe about the roles of men and women in relation to one another. If we espouse a complementarian view of the Trinity, our convictions will likely look different from someone who espouses an egalitarian view.

☻ Respond

Review the descriptions of egalitarianism and complementarianism on pages 24-28. Which school of thought is closest to your convictions about the Trinity? Explain your answer.

What valid truths might the opposite side do well at emphasizing? For instance, if you consider yourself a complementarian, you could point out that egalitarians accurately grasp the equal spiritual value of men and women.

_____

_____

Read through the outline of the Matriarchal to Patriarchal stances on pages 29-34. Which category most closely aligns with your personal convictions? What aspects of that viewpoint caused you to choose it? Download the Theological Cheat Sheet at KadiCole.com/Resources to explore this more fully.

_____

_____

_____

_____

Which category most closely aligns with your church as a whole? Explain your answer.

_____

_____

_____

_____

If there is a gap between your convictions and those of your church, how does this make you feel? Are there potential downsides to this? What about upsides?

_____

_____

_____

_____

Kadi writes, "Although this may open up some uncomfortable dialogue, the female leaders in your church need you to bring clarity and consistency to these issues." Below, write out a prayer to God, committing to pursue truth and to have those difficult, necessary conversations. Ask Him for His wisdom and guidance as you pursue conviction and clarity.

_____

_____

_____

_____

BEST PRACTICE #3:

💡 Big Idea

The marketplace holds valuable lessons for women. Many professionals bring valuable contributions to the ministry. However, many women don't know how to bridge this gap and enter into a leadership role in the church. It's our responsibility to value and equip them.

📖 Read

Chapter 3 in *Developing Female Leaders*

🔍 Reflect and Discuss

Women who attend our churches have a wide variety of marketplace expertise. From attorneys to counselors, they have incredible skill and experience to share with our ministries.

📝 Respond

Who are some of the marketplace women you admire? What do they do? How do they influence others? What skills or values do they exemplify?

_____

_____

_____

_____

If you're a woman in the marketplace, how has your experience there added wisdom and value to your life?

_____

_____

_____

_____

Kadi gives practical tips for onboarding marketplace leaders into your ministry. The first is to make sure you hire only great female leaders. How can you ensure that your team reserves these positions for competent women?

_____

_____

_____

_____

Often, men and women are given identical jobs with different titles. This leaves women at a disadvantage. Have you encountered a situation like this before?

_____

_____

_____

_____

How do you think a difference in title affects a woman's perception of herself? What about others' perceptions of her?

_____

_____

_____

_____

Fair payment for women seems like a given; sadly, women are often paid less than men for the exact same work. Do you think the church can begin to in-fluence the culture on this subject?

_____

_____

_____

_____

🏆 Reflect and Discuss

"Regardless of your stance on a woman teaching the message, if you want her to be able to lead well in your church, she needs to have regular opportunities to be in front during weekend services."

📝 Respond

How have you seen other churches do this well? How do they empower women without crossing their theological lines?

_____

_____

_____

_____

How is your church doing in this area? Do women have a visible and influential role on Sunday mornings?

_____

_____

_____

_____

What could your church do to ensure that women are acknowledged and supported by both staff and the congregation?

_____

_____

_____

_____

✇ Reflect and Discuss

"Any professional who transitions into ministry will need guidance, and women are no exception. But since there are fewer role models and more difficult dynamics, you'll have to be more intentional."

📑 Respond

What guidance do you think is necessary for people coming from the market-place into the ministry?

_____

_____

_____

_____

For women specifically, what extra measures or help is important to make them feel at home and prepared?

_____

_____

_____

_____

What support do you believe churches should offer to spouses and families of ministry leaders?

_____

_____

_____

_____

How can we avoid setting women up on a "glass cliff" where they are taking on more difficult projects or greater leadership risks?

_____

_____

_____

_____

Integrate Spiritual Formation and Leadership Development

💡 Big Idea

A woman's spiritual formation and leadership development are often separated. It's common for male leadership retreats or programs to focus on deep spiritual content, while women's programs center more around "girl time" and feel-good messages. Defining leadership, and connecting it to our identity in Christ, is crucial for female leaders in the church.

📖 Read

Chapter 4 in *Developing Female Leaders*

🎙 Reflect and Discuss

It's imperative that we integrate development and spirituality for women. Practically, that looks like investing in them as leaders while simultaneously affirming their identity in Christ.

📝 Respond

What does the word "integration" mean to you? Define it in one or two sentences.

_____

_____

_____

_____

How do you think the church has separated spiritual formation and leadership development for women?

_____

_____

_____

_____

Have you seen any churches that integrate these well? If so, how specifically do they do this?

_____

_____

_____

_____

⚲ Reflect and Discuss

Kadi interviewed several women who gave testimonies of their time at women's retreats, conferences, or events. Although they appreciated many aspects of these events, for women with leadership gifts these experiences often left them longing for something more.

📰 Respond

Whether or not you've attended a women's church gathering, it's likely you've been exposed to teaching directed towards female church members. What's your primary impression of these events?

_____

_____

_____

_____

What positive attributes have you seen in women's events? Have you heard testimonies of fellowship and healing from these spaces?

_____

_____

_____

_____

Have you encountered any accounts of confusion, hurt, or lack of fulfillment from women's events?

_____

_____

_____

_____

Why do you think some women's events tend to downplay leadership development?

_____

_____

_____

_____

♀ Reflect and Discuss

Defining leadership is key to pursuing all that God has called each of us to be. Many people have a hazy picture of what true, Biblical leadership actually includes. Because of this, Kadi outlines a basic summary on pages 61-62. Take a moment to read over these points, and reflect on how they apply to you personally.

📝 Respond

Every Christian, male or female, is called to be a spiritual leader. Leadership is the ability to influence someone for change. According to God's Word, what influence are you called to have on the world around you?

_____

_____

_____

_____

Leadership can be found in both natural gifts and learned skill sets. Think about your talents, upbringing, and experience. What natural gifts do you possess that can serve to influence others? What learned skills have you developed?

_____

_____

_____

_____

🎙 Reflect and Discuss

Sometimes women leaders don't possess the stereotypical "female gifts" such as hospitality, mercy, helps, and shepherding. This can create confusion as to whether they're enough as a ministry leader. However, our main source of identity isn't drawn from gender stereotypes, but from our identity in Christ!

📝 Respond

What spiritual gifts have you discovered in yourself? Would you say any of these are stereotypically female (or male)?

_____

_____

_____

_____

Assessing our gifts, and those of our church leaders, empowers us to serve more effectively in our sweet spots. God designed us the way we are for His purposes! How can you help those in your church realize and live out their spiritual giftings?

_____

_____

_____

_____

Review the list of "Identity in Christ" struggles on pages 66-67. Which of these, if any, do you struggle with currently? If your struggle isn't on this list, write it out.

_____

_____

_____

_____

Our gifts and talents weren't meant to be developed in a vacuum. God designed the Body of Christ to refine and encourage itself! We need Biblical community to grow. How can you take practical steps initiate, and maintain, healthy relationships in your life?

_____

_____

_____

_____

Dr. Henry Cloud is quoted at the end of Chapter 4: "There is no such thing as our 'spiritual life' and then our 'real life.' It is all one." In your own words, explain what this quote means to you. Does this thought influence the way you think about your daily life?

_____

_____

_____

_____

Be an "Other"

💡 Big Idea

Relationships make all the difference in our lives. Mentors, sponsors, and coaches play integral roles in our journey. For women in ministry, these supportive figures make a huge difference.

📖 Read

Chapter 5 in *Developing Female Leaders*

🔎 Reflect and Discuss

We all have people in our past and present who invested in us. They may be family, neighbors, or even people we meet by accident! None of us can reach our full potential alone—we need others.

📝 Respond

Who are the top three people who have influenced your life for the better? List them below, and write a bit about how they've helped you become who you are today.

_____

_____

_____

_____

Have you been able to invest in others lately? Make a list of those you are currently investing in, or those you aim to know better. How could God use you to develop these people?

_____

_____

_____

_____

God literally wired our brains to need others. Neuroscience tells us that true growth can "only happen in the context of truly connected relationships." How does it make you feel to know that God designed you to be in lifelong fellowship with others—that you weren't meant to do this life alone?

_____

_____

_____

_____

♀ Reflect and Discuss

Kadi outlines three primary categories of relationships that play huge roles in female leaders' development. They are male mentors, male sponsors, and female coaches. Review the basic descriptions of each one, and think about how that category brings something unique to the table.

📝 Respond

Male mentors identify expectations for rising female leaders. They help women develop the right competencies to move forward. If you're a female, do you have any male mentors in your life?

_____

_____

_____

_____

Have you seen male mentors invest in others around you? How did they do so, specifically?

_____

_____

_____

_____

If you're a man, what practical steps could you take to begin to mentor the women in your workplace?

_____

_____

_____

_____

What struggles or pushback might we encounter if we encourage the work-place mentorship between men and women? How can we prepare for this friction ahead of time?

_____

_____

_____

_____

Male sponsors are personal champions who help open up opportunities for women. These men advocate for advancements and pay raises, and have concrete influence when it comes to the women they support. If you're a female, do you have any male sponsors in your life?

_____

_____

_____

Have you seen male sponsors actively support and promote women around you? How did they go about doing this, specifically?

_____

_____

_____

_____

If you're a man, what practical steps can you begin to take to sponsor women in your workplace?

_____

_____

_____

_____

This step is crucial, because, while so many are talking about gender quality, a much smaller circle of people is actually acting on these principles. Do you think sponsors may face even more challenges than mentors? Explain your answer.

_____

_____

_____

_____

Female coaches are women who are present for the journey of other women. There's a part of this journey that's uniquely female, and it's best to have a coach that truly understands. If you're a female, do you currently have any coaches in your life?

_____

_____

_____

_____

If you have coaches, how did you find those people? If you don't have any coaches in your life currently, what steps could you take to find some?

_____

_____

_____

_____

If you're a male, what practical steps could you take to encourage female relationships in your workplace? How can you champion and connect women around you?

_____

_____

_____

_____

☙ Reflect and Discuss

"Many female leaders are reluctant to reach out for help and support...as a church, supporting your female leaders at all levels of the organization with time and budget to receive leadership coaching is a wonderful, and relatively inexpensive, way to invest in their individual development."

🖹 Respond

How do you think churches can communicate the value they place on female leaders? What benefits and investments will show women they are wanted and needed?

_____

_____

_____

_____

How might an outside coach or mentor be able to help your female leaders in a fresh, unique way?

_____

_____

_____

_____

If you're in church leadership, it's likely you know some other ministry leaders who specialize in coaching and spiritual development. Which events or speakers might serve your female leaders, inspiring them to take the next step in their development? Make a short list below, and brainstorm how you might connect with these people.

_____

_____

_____

_____

Create an Environment of Safety

💡 Big Idea

Dangerous, inappropriate behaviors are all too real in our society. Church leadership teams absolutely need to protect everyone by having clear procedures and communication on what to do in these scenarios.

📖 Read

Chapter 6 in *Developing Female Leaders*

🏆 Reflect and Discuss

"'It is estimated that more than one-third of women have been sexually harassed or abused at work'...From belittling to full-on sexual harassment and assault, none of these behaviors are acceptable in the family of God."

📝 Respond

God hates abuse and harassment. As Christians, we are called to protect, defend, and bring freedom to those around us. All too often, however, churches are at the center of huge sexual scandals. Why do you think this problem plagues the church as much as it does today?

_____

_____

_____

_____

Do you believe the church is doing a good job of raising awareness in order to prevent these abusive behaviors? Explain your answer.

_____

_____

_____

_____

Take a look at the Billy Graham Rules on pages 95-96? Do you think this is an effective method of keeping believers from falling into these traps?

_____

_____

_____

_____

What positive aspects do the Billy Graham rules possess that could help churches today set boundaries and be held accountable?

_____

_____

_____

_____

What's possibly missing from these rules given our modern-day society and culture?

_____

_____

_____

_____

⚲ Reflect and Discuss

"The more postmodern our society gets and the more unstable the families in which we are raised become, the more confused we are about what healthy relationships are, particularly around the topic of intimacy."

📝 Respond

Why do you think there's an over-emphasis on romantic relationships in the church, and a lack of emphasis on more distanced, social relationships?

_____

_____

_____

_____

What role does culture play in perpetuating the idea that we find ultimate fulfillment in only one kind of bond?

_____

_____

_____

_____

Which of the four relationship categories do you need more of in your life? Which one are you doing well at cultivating?

_____

_____

_____

_____

As leaders, how are we uniquely called to demonstrate love? How does leadership change the paradigm of our relationships?

_____

_____

_____

_____

How do you think the church can create healthy boundaries between leaders so that they don't slip into a "discipleship" mentality?

_____

_____

_____

_____

⚲ Reflect and Discuss

"Creating a safe work environment free from harassment or predatorial behavior by anyone is imperative to the development of both male and female leaders who are godly, healthy, and trustworthy."

📑 Respond

How does the idea of always bringing along two ministry partners mitigate risk? Are there any possible downsides to this policy?

_____

_____

_____

_____

How can your church have more training on purity and self-leadership? How can you emphasize the need for your team to each be spiritually growing at all times?

_____

_____

_____

_____

What clear boundaries need to be established and reinforced in your church office?

_____

_____

_____

_____

How can church leaders potentially abuse freedoms such as alcohol, medication, and other aspects of self-care? What does the Bible have to say about how we use our freedoms (check out 1 Corinthians 6:12-20, Romans 6, and Hebrews 12:1-12)?

_____

_____

_____

_____

What boundaries have you enacted in your life to keep you from abusing your freedoms?

_____

_____

_____

_____

Every church needs to have a clear process and person for reporting harassment, abuse, or crime. If your church has a clear policy, write it below. If you haven't yet formed or clarified your policy, write your thoughts on what it should include below.

_____

_____

_____

_____

Upgrade Your People Practices

💡 Big Idea

It's difficult to realize, and admit to, our biases. However we need to address them to ensure our female leaders receive equal pay, accurate titles, and appropriate benefits. We must work not just to fill quotas or make token gestures, but to honestly and inclusively assign responsibility and authority.

📖 Read

Chapter 7 in *Developing Female Leaders*

🎙 Reflect and Discuss

"Our brains are made to notice patterns, make generalizations, and create categories. It's what helps us navigate our complex world and make sense of all the information coming at us during a given day. It makes us efficient, smart, and decisive. But it can also set us up to overgeneralize, even when we think we are doing the good or right thing. This is known as unconscious bias or implicit bias, and it shows up in real-life situations all the time."

📝 Respond

Why do you think believers sometimes have a difficult time seeing and admitting our biases?

_____

_____

_____

_____

Kadi lists a few historical examples of times when the Church's bias led to pain, sin, and hatred towards others. Can you think of any present-day examples of this, in either your personal life or the world at-large?

_____

_____

_____

_____

Has the Lord ever revealed a bias in your heart? How did that experience change the way you thought and acted?

_____

_____

_____

_____

In your church, what biases do you see? How do you think the church can effectively address these biases?

_____

_____

_____

_____

🎙️ Reflect and Discuss

"Facing the reality of how we recruit and hire, pay and support, and develop and assess both our male and female workers can give us unique insight into our culture's blind spots and our own unconscious biases."

📝 Respond

Equal pay for equal work seems like a given. However, research shows us that women get paid significantly less for the same work as men. What has your experience been with this reality? Have you, or a loved one, experienced this firsthand?

_____

_____

_____

_____

What "leftover" hiring practices from a previous time may be tainting your church?

_____

_____

_____

_____

Giving accurate titles to women is also essential for them to carry out their responsibilities effectively. How can churches identify women with positions of responsibility in ways that also take into account the churches' different theological views? (e.g. "director" versus "pastor")

_____

_____

_____

What do you think it does to a woman's self-esteem and confidence when we accurately title the work she is doing?

_____

_____

_____

_____

Appropriate benefits are the third element Kadi discusses in hiring practices. What specific benefits and conditions do you believe women in ministry leadership positions should receive?

_____

_____

_____

_____

How do benefits boost the morale—and long-term loyalty—of female leaders? Do you have any personal experience with this?

_____

_____

_____

_____

Kadi writes, "In my experience, one of the critical elements missing for most women, especially women on church staffs or in women-based ministries, is honest and constructive feedback." Have you found this observation to be true? Why or why not?

_____

_____

_____

_____

How does false "niceness," or a refusal to discuss areas for improvement, actually disable ministry leaders?

_____

_____

_____

_____

🎙 Reflect and Discuss

"When you get clear on how you want things to look in the future, figuring out what to look at and start measuring today becomes a lot easier."

📝 Respond

Take a look at the metrics presented on pages 135-139. Which of these metrics do you think your church has done a good job studying and evaluating?

_____

_____

_____

_____

Are there any metrics you'd like to pay more attention to in your church (or ratios you feel are not properly balanced)?

_____

_____

_____

_____

⏺ Reflect and Discuss

"'Shared leadership' can be harder in large team environments, where it is more challenging to understand who actually works for the church, what their roles are, and to whom to go for which concern."

📄 Respond

How do you think your church does in caring for the spouses and families of its leaders? Explain your answer.

_____

_____

_____

_____

Which family members play a significant role in your ministry? How do they go about this without being on staff?

_____

_____

_____

_____

How can churches helpfully define boundaries for family members and support teams, while still honoring and acknowledging their contributions?

_____

_____

_____

_____

When it comes down to it, we mustn't do women any undue favors. Neither can we discriminate against them solely based on gender. Equality means that our people practices must be aligned with our biblical convictions about ministry. Write out any final thoughts you have about your church's practices, how they have changed, and how they can change moving forward to ensure this is the case for your church.

_____

_____

_____

_____

Upgrade Your People Practices

💡 Big Idea

The culture of a place dictates what people, male or female, will feel comfortable doing in that space. To change our culture, we must focus on shifting our language, boundaries, and symbols. This is a process that can't be rushed.

📖 Read

Chapter 8 in *Developing Female Leaders*

🎙 Reflect and Discuss

Women who are "going first" in ministry often run up against the conditioned beliefs we've discussed. These reservations keep them from fully stepping into all they have available to them. The transition into a new culture can be painful for female leaders.

📝 Respond

Why is culture more essential than vision, strategy, or resources?

_____

_____

_____

In what ways are male leaders in the church often unaware of the cultural characteristics that hold women back from stepping into their full callings? Why do you think this is the case?

Think about a time when you, or a loved one, had a ministry opportunity open up. What reservations, or concerns, made you hesitate to take (or even reject) the opportunity?

Reflect and Discuss

"The organizations that have made the most progress in helping female leaders develop and contribute to their church bodies have strategically and methodically taken on their culture."

Respond

What effects have words and language had on you as a female believer?

Reflect on the last few months of your life. Are there destructive words, or patterns of speaking, that you're convicted about?

_____

_____

_____

_____

How can your church make space for everyone on the ministry team to safely share their perspectives, while still maintaining its authority structure?

_____

_____

_____

_____

Boundaries is the second aspect of culture we must address. In your church, what behavioral boundaries exist—not only for your ministry team, but for your congregation?

_____

_____

_____

_____

Are you communicating these boundaries in a way that a first-time guest would be able to quickly understand where your lines are? Explain your answer.

_____

_____

_____

_____

Kadi writes, "Symbols and icons carry deep meanings and can communicate much more effectively than words alone." What power do you believe symbols hold in your church? How have you seen them used and misused?

_____

_____

_____

_____

How can we use symbols to include female leaders in our ministries in a way that empowers and acknowledges them?

_____

_____

_____

_____

⚑ Reflect and Discuss

"As with any kind of initiative or cultural shift, progress can sometimes feel slow. It is important to keep this vision alive in your teams and in your church."

📝 Respond

Perhaps you've begun to make changes based on the things you've studied and read about in this book and in Scripture. Have you run into any roadblocks, or noticed that things are moving more slowly than you'd prefer?

_____

_____

_____

_____

How can delays or a slow pace of change actually make the changes more effective in the long run?

_____

_____

_____

_____

Why might those on your leadership team be averse to the changes you want to make? What valid points might they have that would benefit your team?

_____

_____

_____

_____

Next Steps and Final Thoughts for Churches

💡 Big Idea

Once you've refined your Scriptural stance, it's time to enact the appropriate changes. These ten suggestions on where to begin shifting your church culture will help you begin to flip the script for your female leaders.

📖 Read

Chapter 9 in *Developing Female Leaders*

🎙 Reflect and Discuss

By listening well, defining reality, and setting your vision, you can create a setting for female leaders to be confident in who they are and their roles in your church.

📝 Respond

What questions can you begin asking the women in your church to acquire a better understanding?

_____

_____

_____

_____

Make a list of some female leaders you want to sit down with for "listening sessions" in the near future. Include any ideas of activities or settings that could accompany these meetings.

_____

_____

_____

_____

Based on the previous notes you've made on best people practices, list some ways your church can concretely define its reality—beliefs, culture, and vision—for your female leaders.

_____

_____

_____

_____

What will your church look like ten years from now? Write out your church's vision, and the goals that will help you get there.

_____

_____

_____

_____

🏆 Reflect and Discuss

Finding and leading individuals who champion female leaders is crucial to giving your women a visible platform.

📝 Respond

It's most effective to have one person on your staff who champions female leadership. Who would this be in your church, and why did you select this person?

_____

_____

_____

_____

How can you ensure that you discuss theological changes and reservations with your leadership team? How can you accommodate their shift in culture and understanding?

_____

_____

_____

_____

What are some concrete ways that you can make women visible and give them platforms at your church?

_____

_____

_____

_____

🔎 Reflect and Discuss

Finally, when we clean up our bad habits, recruit the people in our pews who have value to offer, and place them based on their giftings, we set our leaders up to succeed.

📝 Respond

What bad habits does your church need to clean up when it comes to biases and actions? What about you personally?

_____

_____

_____

_____

How can you begin to incorporate stories and messages into your church programs that portray women in a positive light?

_____

_____

_____

_____

How can you practically reach out to experienced, wise women in your congregation who have something to offer to your ministry?

_____

_____

_____

_____

How can you work to ensure your staff has a mind-set that there's "room for
everyone," and encourage mentor relationships for your female leaders?

_____

_____

_____

_____

In your own words, explain why gift-based ministry placement is so important
for both individuals and the church.

_____

_____

_____

_____

Do you sense the conversation shifting? Do you see hopeful signs in churches around the world today? If so, recount some of the good signs you see. If not, what can you do personally to make a change right where you are today?

_____

_____

_____

_____

Best Practices for Female Leaders

💡 Big Idea

By implanting these five best practices, female leaders can set themselves up to succeed, and utilize their gifts fully for the kingdom of God. No matter what others are doing around you, you can get started developing your leadership and fully fulfilling all your callings.

📖 Read

Chapter 11 in *Developing Female Leaders*

🔍 Reflect and Discuss

Kadi writes, "When everyone I felt I needed was stripped away and it was just me and God, I began to understand in my deepest soul from where my strength really comes." Until we get clear on our callings, everything else we undertake will be unfocused and unfruitful in some way.

📝 Respond

Are you regularly feasting on God's Word to refine your sense of identity? How often are you in the Word right now?

_____

_____

_____

_____

Does the idea of being a misfit resonate to you? Why or why not? Do you agree with the idea that Christianity by definition requires us to be misfits?

_____

_____

_____

_____

Understanding your gifts enables you to utilize them to their full capacity in worshipping God and serving others. If you know some of your top spiritual gifts, write them below. If not, take time to take a spiritual gifts test, and record your results.

_____

_____

_____

_____

Kadi writes, "God has ordained ground for you to claim, places for you to be victorious, and a positioning in which you will bless and influence your world." How can you ensure that you don't hold back, like the Israelites, and miss out on all that He has for you?

_____

_____

_____

_____

☻ Reflect and Discuss

Best Practice #2 for female leaders is to know our environment. Knowing whether our hearts are in alignment with God's Word, and whether our beliefs line up with those of our leadership, will provide clarity as we navigate ministry struggles. Are we able to, in good conscious, submit to our current leadership?

📝 Respond

Is your heart right in terms of respectfully submitting to those in authority over you? Do you ever find yourself struggling to remain humble in this area?

_____

_____

_____

_____

It's nearly impossible to fully agree on every subject with another human being. That being said, it's essential that those in your ministry agree on certain fundamental Christian truths. Do your essential beliefs line up with those in authority over you?

_____

_____

_____

_____

What differences in belief do you have with your church leaders?

_____

_____

_____

_____

Given the similarities and differences in your beliefs, do you believe you're able to follow and submit to the leadership where you are right now? Explain your answer.

_____

_____

_____

_____

🎙 Reflect and Discuss

There is room for everyone at Christ's table. Likewise, there is room for everyone in the ministry of the church. As female leaders, we must make sure we keep this mindset when it comes to working with others.

📄 Respond

Have you struggled with a "Queen Bee" mentality at any time in the past? What was the driving force behind that spirit? Competitiveness? Fear? Lack of self-esteem?

_____

_____

_____

_____

Do you ever feel like you have to walk the road of female leadership alone? Where do you think this message came from? What does Scripture have to say about this?

_____

_____

_____

_____

🎙 Reflect and Discuss

Playing cards is a tempting, yet non-rewarding, tactic that some women use to garner attention or sympathy. It's essential that we don't discredit ourselves by making excuses, but lead with simplicity and honesty.

📝 Respond

Which cards have you played in the past? What motivated you to play those cards?

_____

_____

_____

_____

In your own words, explain why playing cards actually hurts female leaders more than it benefits them.

_____

_____

_____

_____

🎙 Reflect and Discuss

A support system is perhaps the most essential element of stepping into your full potential as a leader in ministry. We all need brothers and sisters in Christ to refine and encourage us. Make sure your system is strong and vibrant.

📝 Respond

Who do you have in your current support system? How do these individuals bring you closer to Christ and to your full potential as a leader?

_____

_____

_____

_____

Do you consider yourself good at asking for help? Why or why not?

_____

_____

_____

_____

Is it easier for you to ask for help from men or from women? How could asking for help from the opposite gender provide you with fresh insight?

_____

_____

_____

_____

As you finish reading this book, do any of the "Words of Encouragement" from Kadi's interviewees resonate with you? Write them below.

_____

_____

_____

_____

What is the one thing you feel convicted and encouraged to do now that you've finished this study? Pray, and commit to asking God (and others) for the strength and help to do it.

_____

_____

_____

_____